The Little Book

of

100 Moments

The Little Book
of
100 Moments

A co-created wellness and wisdom project

Curated by Jonathan Dean

Created with love from 50+ contributors
Foreword by Chandler Phillips
Designed by Mel Shields

979-8-9877411-8-4 (paperback)

Library of Congress Catalog Card Number: 0000-0000

Jonathan Dean (Author)

Contents

————

Nurture *Chapter 3*   69

Love *Chapter 4*

Foreword

a

p   e

u

s

s   t

r   e

e

l

r   a   e

b

e   t

h

listen.

to this body   earth
to this breath   air
to this spirit   sun
to this blood   water

listen   &   feel
listen   &   wonder
listen   &   dream
listen   &   remember

listening is the act of being with

surrendering the self to be
                           opened

                                        broken

                                                built

                                                        lost

                                                                loved

listen
(to these pages)

what do you hear?

———

written by a Black body, atop a white page, on a Brown and bloodied land of Turtle Island—chandler phillips

What is a Moment?

Noun
A brief period of time. A pause. Stillness.
A period of heightened awareness and emotion.
To live in the moment. To act without worrying about the future.
Fully focused and present in the experience of now.

In this book, a Moment
is a combination of words offered
to the world.

—

Moments can be:

- A collection of original words

- A poem

- Words of wisdom

- A lesson learned

- An inspiring message

- An affirmation

Curator's Notes

To the 54 contributors

With love and gratitude, I say thank you. I would not be who I am today without each of you. It is an honor to amplify the voices and perspectives of so many thoughtful and creative humans.

Together, our Moments create a web of wisdom for future generations to hold and carry. May we continue to experience earth's tastes in a quest for abundant joy, love, peace, and understanding.

To the readers

This book was crafted with love, care, and hope for a brighter future. I hope you find a bit of your own story in these pages as we collectively heal ourselves and the planet.

For the dreamers out there, this project is proof that you, too, can bring your ideas to life if you believe you can.

On the Idea Gardens

With support from Dr. Hava Rose, we've created open spaces with journaling prompts at the end of each chapter. This is your opportunity to pick up the pen and create your own personal Moments.
To dream.
To reflect.
To design the world you want to live in.

On Tending the Garden

In this section I share personal insights on my approach to self-care, home-care, and earth-care.

On the 100 Moments of Media

A curated collection of inspirations and influences that lead to the creation of this book.

Who wrote which Moment?

In this book, contributors either:
1) share their own original words
2) feature another person's words

In either case, the original author of each Moment is listed at the bottom of the Moment's page. To see the full list of contributors, flip to page 207.

On my contributions

As the curator of the project, I personally contributed 43 of the 100 Moments. 11 of them are a sampling of my original poems and the remaining 32 feature words from inspiring leaders.

On poetry as a medium

For me, poetry is the process of composting emotions into language we can understand and share.

Writing is healing and healing is power.

As Abraham Joshua Heschel said, "words create worlds."

Let's take a walk in the garden.
—xoxo Jonathan Dean

Continue the conversation and view video versions of the Moments on Instagram @_thelittlebook

Chapter One

The Seed

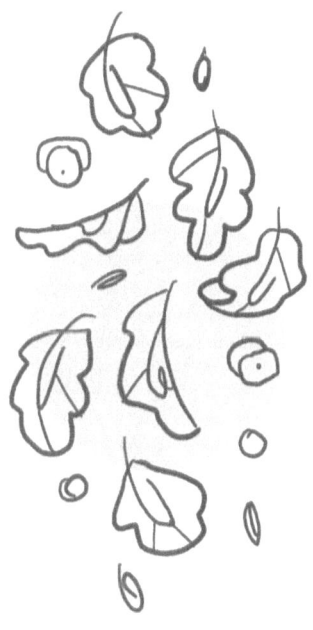

Love Letter to Comfrey
Part 1

To the wonderful Comfrey plant -

I am a seed with big dreams and I'm embarking on a journey to discover my purpose. I write to you because I seek your guidance and the wisdom of the natural world. Your deep roots, beautiful flowers, and perennial renewal cycles are my inspiration.

I hope to one day flower like you but today all I see is darkness and I am scared. Scared that it's too late for our beautiful planet. Scared by how much fear can tear us apart.

Scared for a day when fresh water doesn't flow and healthy food doesn't grow.

Can you teach me the lessons of the natural world as I embark on this journey?

with love,

Jonathan the Seed

Moment 1
The Seed

If I am a seed
eventually I must
burst from my shell
into the darkness of the soil that nurtures me
out into the world
to feel the warmth
of the sun
on the face
of my leaves
if I am a seed.

—Zoya Yaseka

Moment 2

Roots

Our fruits are only as strong as our roots.

—Thenjiwe Tameika McHarris

Moment 3

In

Breathing in, I calm my body.

—*Thích Nhất Hạnh*

Moment 4
Out

Breathing out, I smile.

—*Thích Nhất Hạnh*

Moment 5
Upstream

Attention is the beginning of devotion.

—*Mary Oliver*

Moment 6

Anchor

My breath is an anchor to the present.

—Original author is unknown

Moment 7

Power

A relaxed body is the most powerful body.

—Adrienne Maree Brown

Moment 8
Closer

Sit comfortably.
Work tends to fade, "x" can wait.

Close your eyes.
Dim your expectations, if only for a while.

Wait about a half a minute.
Notice thoughts coming and going.
Welcome quiet when it seeps in.

Begin thinking the Mantra.
Just like any other thought
it will bubble up and away and again.

Afterwards, emerge.
Take a beat.
Two are better.

Is it a moment?
It is tangibly closer.

—Dan Kershner, with inspiration from
Bob Roth and Ralph Emmerich

Moment 9
Seek Stillness

The answers lie on the other side of boredom
exhale slowly
enjoy this moment
joy awoken.
The answers lie on the other side of boredom.

—Jonathan Dean

Moment 10
Bloom

And then the day came when the risk to remain tight in a bud was more painful than the risk to blossom.

—*Anaïs Nin*

Prompts
Idea Garden Part 1

Welcome to your first Idea Garden!
At the end of each chapter you will arrive at these spaces for you to
pick up the pen and create your own Moments.

Find a comfortable seat and enjoy a deep breath.
The soil is waiting for you to bloom.

Imagine you are a seed.

What are you hoping to cultivate in your life right now?

What is something that helps you slow down?

What is a fear you are currently holding?

Where do you want to feel more connected in your life?

A space to doodle and draw

Chapter Two

Blossom

Love Letter to Comfrey
Part 2

Hello Comfrey,

I write to you with excitement as this morning I stretched my first
roots into the darkness. I know they are tiny, but I hope with your
guidance I will one day unite with the light and find my truth.

I've been observing your many talents and you continue to inspire
me. Like when your roots extend deep into the ground to un-
earth and distribute nitrogen, phosphorus, and potassium with
the world. Or when your life-giving leaves decompose to rebuild
troubled soils.

I want to share love like you share nutrients.

I want to support others on their journey.

I want to leave the world in a better place.

Do you have a secret to staying rooted amid the chaos?

Jonathan

Moment 11
Trust

My intention is to trust.

My body has a holotropic agenda.
Just like sunflowers are photo-tropic
(*etymology*: "turning towards light")
I am turning towards wholeness.
Oh yes, I am. That is my nature.

ٱلْحَمْدُ لِلّٰه

—*Mathama B.*

Moment 12
Light

There is always light,
if only we're brave enough to see it.
If only we're brave enough to be it.

—*Amanda Gorman*

Moment 13
Flow

There is a flow of nurturing which drives life.
No one is fated for drought.

Though when you grow up thirsty, you harden.
When you harden, your veins cannot receive the love
when it trickles onto you.

So stay soft, as soft as you can.
And if you find yourself hardened,
work out each knot.
Drink water. Pray for rain.

One day, no tears will fall on your peaceful breath.
You'll smile in a sun shower,
and feel love in your blood.

—*Gia Athanasia*

Moment 14

Vulnerability as Courage

Vulnerability is not winning or losing;
it's having the courage to show up and be seen when we have
no control over the outcome.

Vulnerability is not weakness;
it's our greatest measure of courage.

—Brené Brown

Moment 15
Fear

Named must your fear be, before banish it you can.

—*Yoda*

Moment 16
The Way

The obstacle is the way.

—*Ryan Holiday*

Moment 17
Intrinsic Value

Everything you learn may not be immediately actionable
but all knowledge is intrinsically valuable.

—*Shadman Uddin*

Moment 18

The Truth

That which can be destroyed by the truth should be.

—*P. C. Hodgell*

Moment 19

Discovery

Increase in me that wisdom which discovers my truest interests.
Strengthen my resolutions to perform what wisdom dictates...

—*Benjamin Franklin*

Moment 20
Read and Write

If you're overthinking, *write*
If you're underthinking, *read*

—Alex Wiec

Moment 21
Belief

He who says he can, and he who says he can't... are both correct.

—Confucius

Moment 22
Self-Love Rules

The relationship you have with yourself is the most important
relationship you'll ever have.

Make sure you water yourself as much as you water others.

Set your boundaries and remember that "no" is a full sentence too.

—*Melissa Alam*

Moment 23

Imposter?

Do you ever surprise yourself?
Or maybe even scare yourself?
You look around and you look back.
It's hard to reconcile how far you've come.
Do you belong?
Do you deserve to be here?
How did you get so lucky?
When you're always focused on the next step,
The next milestone,
The next promotion,
You can forget that you envisioned this.
You prayed for this.
You spoke this into existence.
So you can't forget to keep moving.
Because our deepest fear is not that we are inadequate.
Our deepest fear is that we are powerful
Beyond measure.
So take up space.
Recognize your unique brilliance.
And make sure they put respect on
Your Name.

—*Darren Douglas with inspiration from Marianne Williamson*

Moment 24

Be Yourself

Always be yourself, because your alternate versions
are frankly, worse.

—Sebastian De Beurs

Moment 25
Life

Live without pretending,
Love without depending,
Listen without defending,
Speak without offending.

—*Aubrey Drake Graham*

Moment 26

Still I Rise

Just like moons and like suns,
With the certainty of tides,
Just like hopes springing high,
Still I'll rise.

—Maya Angelou

Prompts
Idea Garden Part 2

Welcome to your next Idea Garden!
It's time to dream, wander, and grow.

What is giving you energy today?

What is something you are currently overthinking?

Name a moment when you trusted yourself.

If anything is possible, who would you be?

A space to doodle and draw

Chapter Three

Nurture

Love Letter to Comfrey
Part 3

Dear Comfrey,

This morning I rose with the sun and saw my first light! I'm excited by this growth but am realizing how much I have yet to learn.

I hope to one day flower like you and find my purpose.

This afternoon I saw you shading the soil to protect vulnerable life from the summer sun.

How do you find the strength to serve others? I hope to hear from you soon.

Jonathan

and Comfrey responds...

Hello my heavenly friend. I appreciate your vulnerability and hope I can help. I'm confident you will one day find your purpose and serve the world but you'll first need to look inward, seek stillness, and care for yourself.

"Faith is the bird that feels the light and sings when the dawn is still dark."[1]

—*Comfrey*

Moment 27

Watering

The seed that doesn't get watered
cannot reveal its ability to bear fruit.

—*Rick Rubin*

Moment 28

The Reminder

Be open & be kind to yourself.

—Garrett Godshall

Moment 29
Rest as Pleasure

In each moment, we are deserving
of rest.
rest is not a luxury; rest does not need
to be earned, only enjoyed.
standing still is not moving backwards:
standing still is being here, now.
standing still is not falling behind; rather,
it is falling into ourselves, into the depth of the present moment.

In each moment, we are deserving
of pleasure.
pleasure is not a luxury; pleasure does not need
to be earned, only enjoyed.
pleasure is not moving backwards.
pleasure is being here, now.
pleasure is not falling behind; rather,
it is falling into ourselves, into the depth of this
pleasurable, present moment.

—Brunson

Moment 30

Patience

Nature does not hurry yet everything is accomplished.

—*Lao Tzu*

Moment 31
Make

Nothing is a mistake. There is no win and no fail.
There is only make.

—*Sister Mary Corita Kent*

Moment 32

Nature as Teacher

Have you ever failed to achieve a goal?
If so, I bet you have succeeded more than you know...

For it is only through trying,
that seeds are even given a chance to sow

With nature as our greatest teacher
We continuously learn to adapt and grow.

—*Matai Blacklock*

Moment 33
Discipline and Freedom

Discipline and freedom seem like opposites.
In reality, they are partners.

Discipline is not a lack of freedom, it is a harmonious relationship
with time. Managing your schedule and daily habits well is a
necessary component to free up the practical and creative capacity
to make great art.

—*Rick Rubin*

Moment 34
Four Thousand Weeks

Stand firm in the face of FOMO because missing out on something - indeed, on almost everything - is basically guaranteed.

Which isn't actually a problem anyway, it turns out, because "missing out" is what makes our choices meaningful in the first place.

—Oliver Burkeman

Moment 35
Grateful

Gratitude will teach you to have less wanting
because what you have will be enough.

—Original author is unknown

Moment 36
Live Light

The accumulation of belongings can restrict your ability to
welcome in change. Live light and be free.

—Bonnie Keiles

Moment 37

Now

Do what you can, with what you've got, where you are.

—Teddy Roosevelt via Squire Bill Widener

Moment 38
Keep Moving

The only thing a person can ever really do is keep moving forward.

—Alyson Noël

Moment 39

The Universe Never Explains Why

We cannot control the fish, only the presence of our line.

—Rick Rubin

Moment 40
Wind

It's helpful to view currents in the culture without feeling obligated to follow the direction of their flow. Instead, notice them in the same connected, detached way you might notice a warm wind. Let yourself move within it, yet not be of it.

—Rick Rubin

Moment 41

Make Your Favorite

You can't second guess, you know? You just have to make your favorite. As long as you're consistently making your favorite, you're gonna be alright

—*Rick Rubin*

Moment 42
Life on Life's Terms

Expectations are the enemy of true enjoyment.

We consciously or unconsciously expect something to be one way, but more often than not, it goes the other way...

To live a life of serenity, enjoy the moment for what it is, and nothing else...set your expectations aside and experience life on life's terms.

—Matt Aragona

Moment 43

Joy

Joy does not simply happen to us. We have to choose joy and keep choosing it every day.

—*Henri Jozef Machiel Nouwen*

Moment 44

Reality Setter vs Trend Setter: Creative Architects Beyond Artistry

I've been closely observing the world around me and reevaluating the concept of creativity.

Creatives aren't limited to those who express themselves artistically; they're more like creative artists. Consider the Founding Fathers of the Declaration of Independence – they didn't just craft words, they shaped the rules that guide our nation. Similarly, I view the framers of the constitution as political creatives. When I start to perceive our society as one built upon the imaginative visions of these creatives, it's truly remarkable. This world is not merely a blank sheet of paper; it's my canvas. I can choose to create the world I envision or conform to someone else's creative "reality." So, I ask you are you the creator of your reality or do you live in someone else's?

As for me... I choose to be the creator of my reality and it's an awesome one!

—*Leonzo Vargas*

Moment 45

Act

The wise man lets go of all results, whether good or bad, and is
focused on the action alone.

—*Vyasa, translated by Stephen Mitchell*

Moment 46
Brave

Be brave with your life,
so others may be brave with theirs.

—Katherine Center

Prompts
Idea Garden Part 3

You are on the path towards abundance.
The future is in your hands.

What is a self-care practice you would like to commit to?
When during your day will you make time for it?

What is something you are grateful for today?

What is a moment in your life that you are proud of?

What is something that is no longer serving you?
Name a boundary you'd like to set for yourself.

A space to doodle and draw

Chapter Four
Love

Love Letter to Comfrey
Part 4

Hello Comfrey,

Thank you for your words. I'm sensing I'm on the right path but I'm scared we're running out of time. Our soil is degraded. We're losing biological and cultural diversity. Our systems are built on extraction and we're forgetting indigenous ways of living that honor the land.

I hear our planet's cries for help but more questions emerge as I try to uncover my purpose.

How am I best suited to support change? How have I benefitted from the current systems in place? Is it too late for me to make a difference?

I need your help and know I can't do this alone.

Jonathan

and Comfrey responds...

*It is never too late to act, but you are correct...**we don't have much time.** There are limits to our planet's resilience.*

The answers lie within so listen with curiosity, surround yourself with love, and you will discover your truth soon.

—*Comfrey*

Moment 47
Change

All that you touch
You Change.
All that you Change
Changes you.

—Octavia E. Butler

Moment 48
Joyful

Joy's power is that small moments can spark big changes.

—Ingrid Fetell Lee

Moment 49

Flowers

The most precious gift we can offer anyone is our presence.
When mindfulness embraces those we love,
they will bloom like flowers.

—*Thích Nhất Hạnh*

Moment 50

Sun

The sun in your face,
quit runnin the race.
Money makes the world go round,
but love makes it all stand still.

—Jonathan Dean

Moment 51
Loyalty

What if you were the flower
and I was the soil?
Loyal to your roots like a family tree.
Love growing wide as the branches be.

—Jonathan Dean

Moment 52
The "Feminine Monarchy"

Many say that honeybees can show us how to live: in sweetness, in beauty and in peacefulness.

The honeybee is a leader, an individual, and one part of a whole.
How curiously she builds
How stoutly her common-good defends
What pleasures she imparts.

Women, more often than men, and for better or for worse, are love's practitioners and a community's bedrock.

Honeybees, in their feminine structure, teach us about community as they protect, sustain and create love with their shared nectar, comb, and honey.

For us, the honeybee guides our communities and shows us love we can see as she wings her way with seemingly careless will. From mount to plane, over lake and winding wave.

A community we must build will remember to praise her wildflowers, cherish her fruits and learn from her peace.

—Claire Rater with inspiration from Thomas Seeley, Bell Hooks, Thomas Smibert, and Charles Butler

Moment 53
Together Forward

Ask not what your community can do for you but what you can do
for your community.

—*Adapted from John F. Kennedy's original words*

Moment 54

The Feeling

Do you feel it, the feeling of feeling the feeling?!?!
Hold onto it until it doesn't serve you any longer
and if it brought you joy pass it on.

—*Carlos Aponte*

Moment 55

Inspire Creativity

You can't teach creativity, you can only inspire people. Focus your
energy towards inspiring and the creativity will flow.

—Bruce Hurowitz

Moment 56

Embrace

Don't try to change the people you love. Then they wouldn't be the
people you fell in love with.

—*Alex Topel*

Moment 57

Perspective

We judge ourselves by our intentions
and others by their behavior.

—Stephen Covey

Moment 58

Listen

Sonder *noun* - the realization that each random passerby is living a life as vivid & complex as your own - with their own routines, dreams, worries, & inherited craziness.

If I'm too caught up with my own thoughts, feelings & emotions - how can I truly help someone else?

Everyone has a story to tell... but are you listening?

—Sly

Moment 59
Beyond Destinations

In life, the value of spending time with true friends consistently outweighs the allure of any destination. Nevertheless, when people and place collide, they forge everlasting memories.

—*Ethan Asher*

Moment 60

Acrylic and Canvas

Life without friends is an empty canvas, devoid of vibrant hues and profound connections.

True friendship reveals itself when we recognize fragments of our own identity in them, a beautiful yet sometimes unsettling revelation.

They are architects of our souls,
Crafting with love and care,
A masterpiece of friendship,
Beyond compare.

So my question to you, who are your friends?

—Kadir Abdi

Moment 61
Service

Even within purpose and serving others,
you still have to serve yourself.

—*Vic Blends*

Moment 62

Breathe

Don't forget to breathe~

—Stonez the Organic

Prompts
Idea Garden Part 4

To guide our dreaming within this Idea Garden, we call on Esther Perel's wise words, "The quality of your life ultimately depends on the quality of your relationships."[2]

How does community show up in your life? Name a community, organization, or group of people that you would like to deepen your connection with this year.

How do you like to be supported?

Name the people that support you most.
Why are you grateful for them?

How can you better support your loved ones this year?
If you aren't sure, ask them how you can support them.

A space to doodle and draw

Chapter Five

Decompose

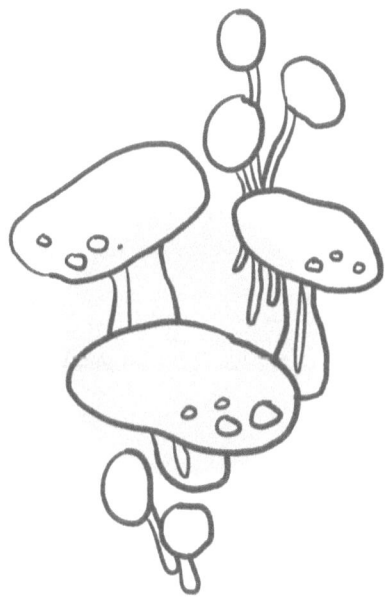

Love Letter to Comfrey
Part 5

Hello Comfrey -

I appreciate your guidance through these challenging times. I wish I could move with the patience of plants and surrender to life's storms as they come and go.

This morning my mom told me about the latest sickness in our family. It seems I have a talent for distracting myself from negative emotions.

I fear impermanence. I'm addicted to my phone. I use the word "should" too much.

I judge myself. I judge others.

And I'm realizing they are one and the same.

This afternoon at the community garden I saw your leaves decomposing into soil-serving mulch. I admire how you graciously support life. Do you have a secret to your continuous cycles of renewal?

and Comfrey responds...

There is no singular secret to blossoming but it starts with having the courage to find faith among fears and hope among tears.

To trust yourself.
To love yourself.
To believe in a brighter tomorrow.

How do you think I've survived the last 2,000+ years? I've persevered through droughts, floods, the rise of machines, and chemical storms all to show you that regeneration is still possible.

Lead with love and we will all flower again. Commit to your truth and you will give others permission to do the same.

The seeds of inner abundance bloom into collective action.

—Comfrey

Moment 63
Feel

We don't practice to feel good, we practice to feel more.

—*Adrienne Maree Brown*

Moment 64
A Prayer

Let my heart break, but only just enough.
I am your silence, your eternal gift.
Eyes open in a breath of wisdom,
wearing the cloak of life lightly
I cannot control the entirety of this compulsion.
In my surrender to release you,
I give myself to the Divine
the breath that inhabits every cell,
Her silence aches as a moment pulses.
Shrouded in a memory, swallowed by a dream,
The wise ones seek the collapse.
Let my heart break, but only just enough.

—Nathalie Shapiro

Moment 65
The Lesson of the Falling Leaves

the leaves believe
such letting go is love
such love is faith
such faith is grace
such grace is god
i agree with the leaves

—*Lucille Clifton*

Moment 66
Fate

This feels like fate
this singular snowflake
Her individuality
Shifted my reality
Wait.
Ground split, earthquake
Tectonic, mistake
Quit joggin my brain waves
Flip fog to a rain day
Grab the pain see what the pain say

—Jonathan Dean

Moment 67
Grief

Grief is just love with no place to go.

—Jamie Anderson

Moment 68
Fear

Sending my love
She's not feeling it
Sharing my words
She's not hearin em
fearin them
not hearin em clear again
the fear is then
At year's end
she steers left
Which path is right
Switch back to fright

I thought love was the light.

—Jonathan Dean

Moment 69

Awareness

Feel the heartbreak, stew in it.
This is a blessing to raise your awareness.

—*Carlos Aponte*

Moment 70

Time

Sand crystals in her hair fell like the hourglass
Time was irrelevant when the hours passed
Wondering how long will this sour last
Cause things were sweet
like a flower to a bee
As we grow apart and see

—Jonathan Dean

Moment 71
Faith

Faith is the bird that feels the light
and sings when the dawn is still dark.

—Rabindranath Tagore

Moment 72
Beauty

I've found beauty in the struggle
Joy in the journey
Peace in the process
I'm okay with the not yet
Better days and the progress

—Jonathan Dean

Moment 73

The Creative Act

There's so much wisdom in nature that when we notice it,
it awakens possibility within us.

It's through communing with nature that we move closer to our
own nature.

—*Rick Rubin*

Moment 74
Begin

Inspiration wilts as reality settles in
The blossoming flower in my mind
A measly plot of dirt in front of me
Toil the soil, I remind myself
Seed in hand, shovel in the other
We begin a new day

—*Cam Lindsay*

Moment 75
Half Full

Always look at the bright side. If not, life passes quickly, is wasted
with negativity, and you miss out on the joy.

—Phyllis Keiles

Moment 76

Care

Music and food
the language of love
tune it and groove
these gifts from above
break bread and bake beats
I'll take streams but I'd rather nourish rivers
love giver, we deliver
farmed and fresh food
the planet charms and tests you
so it's mountains for the blessed view
lemon zest the chef stew
holistic care my next move
holistic care our next move

—Jonathan Dean

Moment 77
Permanent Agriculture

You can solve all the world's problems in a garden.

—*Geoff Lawton*

A learning Moment on... permaculture
Noun

Permaculture or "Permanent Agriculture" is an ecological design methodology that creates symbiotic relationships between plants, animals, materials, and humans. It mimics and regenerates natural ecosystems while creating resilient and sustainable food systems.

Why Permaculture?

Permaculture is one of the golden levers we must pull in our fight against climate change. It has a powerful ability to capture and store rain water, sequester carbon, build soil health, and provide healthy food to ecosystems.

A learning Moment on... swales

What is a Permaculture Swale?

A swale is a shallow trench dug perpendicular along a land's downward slope. As water flows down the landscape, the swale captures and slows it. Plants and trees are positioned around the swale for easy access to both the water and reservoir of nutrients. Over time, groundwater is replenished, soil fertility increases, and the environment nurtures a healthy ecosystem of plants, animals, and people.

A Swale

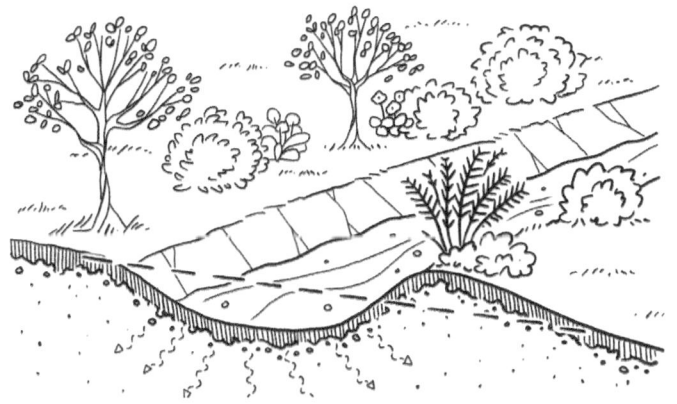

Prompts

Idea Garden Part 5

Welcome back to the Garden! Look how far you've come! Take a
pause and enjoy another deep breath.

Today is a new beginning.

What is something you are currently grieving that you would like to
move through?

Think back to a challenge in your life. What is something you
learned about yourself from that moment?

What are words of wisdom that helped you navigate a
difficult time?

Create an affirmation for yourself. For example, I am patient. I am deserving of love. I have unique gifts to share. Remember this next time you are navigating a challenge or life transition.

A space to doodle and draw

Chapter Six

Renew

Moment 78

Right Now

What can I do to change my life right now?
Thinking of the past always makes me ask how?

What can I do to change my life right now?
Follow my father's voice or follow the crowd?

What can I do to change my life right now?
Judge not another man, we're all on trial

What can I do to change my life right now?
Forgive my family members, I was only a child

What can I do to change my life right now?
Show peace and love to the wretched and the foul

Who? What? When? Where? And How?
I've been so stupid, I get it, the answer is now

—*Kow*

Moment 79

Commitment

Never doubt that a small group of thoughtful, committed citizens
can change the world; indeed, it's the only thing that ever has.

—*Margaret Mead*

Moment 80
Hope

Hope is a verb with the sleeves rolled up.

—David Orr

Moment 81
Steward

Paradoxically, systemic change is a deeply personal endeavour:
our social and economic structures are a product of our way
of thinking.

We must now move from a mindset of extraction to an
understanding of our inextricable connection with nature and a
deep sense of stewardship.

—Christiana Figueres

Moment 82

The Artist's Role

The role of the artist is to make the revolution irresistible.

—Toni Cade Bambara

Moment 83
Go

We have everything we need to make a difference in a timely fashion.

—*Christiana Figueres*

Moment 84

Stains

hesitation will destroy any dream

the future rides on decisions made in the present
but you forgot because back then
you felt alive

it turns out it's better to make the wrong choice
than none at all

the temporary pain of a mistake is like a nosebleed
compared to the drawn out discomfort of the
unknown
the unanswered
a broken nose

and so I'll bleed
I will bleed and bleed and bleed

before I ever break

I hope the world can forgive me
for the stains

—Sarah Kane

Moment 85
Duty

Know what your duty is and do it without hesitation.

—Vyasa, translated by Stephen Mitchell

Moment 86
Limitless

What we're afraid of is not so much our limitations,
but the infinite within us.

—*Nelson Mandela*

Moment 87

Best case you're a roadside attraction on the infinity train.
Worst case, you never got off. Wazow!

—Josie Bulldozer

Moment 88

Come and Go

People, they come and they go.
Things, they come and they go.
Ideas, they come and they go.
Pets, they come and they go.
Everything seems to come, and go.
What truly lasts forever?
Perhaps nothing.
As they say, whatever comes up, must come down.
So maybe we stop worrying about what comes and goes.
And enjoy the ride along the way.

With life, there are no rules for who gets more and who gets less.
Sometimes, those with the most end up with the least.
Other times, those with the least end up with the most.
We will never have all the answers.
Maybe it's just better to learn to enjoy the ride each day.
We begin to stop counting the days behind us.
We start to dream about the days that come ahead of us.
We wake up, live, and rest.
Learn from the past, enjoy today, and dream about tomorrow.
Because after all? We all come.
And we all go.

—Abhinav Sridharan

Moment 89

Part 1:
A Butterfly's Bloom Gone
Too Soon

I
We
Walked up
To a 194 year old Monument
For a 26 year old, 5'2" Giant.
Arrive alone; stand together; leave as one.
A best friend, a former crush, a work acquaintance, me
A raft, a lifeline in a sea of hundreds;
A view blocked by TV cameras
Hunting for meaning, devastating our community
Can you answer "How are you?" with
"I'm as fucked up as you are"
Hugs, bodies, ritual, ceremony, a shout into a dark sky.
A chorus of voices in disharmony, pain,
Woven together in a brief moment.
Devastated, Changed
But one.

—Micky Wolf and Anand K. Macherla

Moment 90
Part 2:
A Butterfly's Hurricane

A
Turn
A rip in our woven ecosystem,
A community embodied by our friend
with a vision of justice and connection bigger than this crime.
A Becoming cut short. A Seeing of relationships as power.
How the butterfly's wings sent this message far and wide.
Of a bright Candle. Courageous and burning, spreading love
Even as its flame becomes smoke
The love, the warmth, the joy connecting us
To this ground all around
Between the family, the friends, the ecosystem is found.
A thousand little candles, sources of heat but
our brightest no longer there.
So we take the wisps and
Burn even
Brighter

—*Micky Wolf and Anand K. Macherla*

Moment 91

Oneness

Every man is born as many men and dies as a single one.
If I take death into my life, acknowledge it, and face it squarely, I
will free myself from the anxiety of death and the pettiness of life -
and only then will I be free to become myself.

—*Martin Heidegger*

Moment 92
Circle

Your sunset is another's sunrise.

—Jonathan Dean

Moment 93
Wisdom

I asked my father who just turned 87, "any regrets?"

He replied, "I would have traveled more."

At the time, it sounded like a standard way an older person would reply. But now that I finally came up for air after 32 years of the grind, I see the wisdom.

It's not just about a plane ride or hotel stay. Or even being in a new city. It's about freedom. Expansion of the mind. Enjoying the day with little or no concern for time. Talking with a stranger with real interest. No rush. No feelings of guilt. No regrets.

I can't wait for the next adventure.

—Eric Keiles

Moment 94

Moments

We do not remember days, we remember moments.

—Cesare Pavese

Moment 95
The Honorable Harvest

Know the ways of the ones who take care of you, so that you may take care of them.
Introduce yourself. Be accountable as the one who comes asking for life. Ask permission before taking. Abide by the answer.

Never take the first. Never take the last. Take only what you need. Take only that which is given.
Never take more than half. Leave some for others. Harvest in a way that minimizes harm.

Use it respectfully. Never waste what you have taken. Share.
Give thanks for what you have been given.
Give a gift, in reciprocity for what you have taken.
Sustain the ones who sustain you and the earth will last forever.

—Robin Wall Kimmerer

Moment 96
Home

The bees will find their own homes,
our role is to plant the flowers to attract them.

—Katrina Day

Moment 97
The Web

Whatever happens to seed affects the web of life.

—*Dr. Vandana Shiva*

Moment 98
Roots

An old man cares for a young tree
Rooted in the future of those unborn
He rests
Blessed
Not stressed by the money that he spent
but the time that he enjoyed

Grandpa, grandpa, why do you always work with your hands?
Mom says it's better to work with your mind.

My son, working with my hands is medicine for the mind
With the wind on my spine
Intertwined with the sky
I forget about time
and trading it

You see my son, nature grounds me
And with my hands in the soil, I am reminded
of the ashes of those that have come before me
And the seeds that have yet to bloom

— *Jonathan Dean*

Moment 99
Heaven

Breath in. The Kingdom of Heaven is available to me now. Breath out. Smile. Breath in. I am alive. Breath out.

—*Caroline Lutkewitte*

Prompts
Idea Garden Part 6

As plants decompose and return to the soil, they pass life on to make way for new abundance.

What is something you would like to welcome into your life?

What is something you would like to pass on to future generations?

What brings you joy?   What are your unique abilities?

What are the similarities between your notes in these two columns?

What is a change you hope to see in this world?
How can you be part of it?

A space to doodle and draw

Final
Love Letter to Comfrey

Hello Comfrey,

I write today to say thank you. Your teachings and the lessons of the natural world are my forever inspiration.

Your support has helped me discover that my purpose actually lies right next to you in the garden.
To steward the soil and care for all those that depend on its life.
To build a community of compassionate and loving individuals.
To focus on myself first so I can share love and serve the collective.

I write today to say thank you.
Your deep roots are my guiding light.
Your nutrient-dense leaves are a reminder that generosity ripples.
Your healthy seeds are a blueprint for future generations.

Thanks to you, I know that wilting is a necessary part of renewal.
Thanks to you, I'm learning to accept what I cannot control.
Thanks to you, I know that love is infinite.

and Comfrey responds...

Of course, Jonathan. You are ready. Your moment is now.

The collective awakening is upon us so get to work, commit to action, and together our flowers will fruit forever.

To the blooming seeds of tomorrow, life and love is now in your hands so I ask you...

What is your truth and what will you do with it?

Epilogue

Tending the Garden

In our eternal quest to heal our planet, we must first heal ourselves. The section below shares a glimpse look into how I approach the delicate and interconnected balance of self-care, home-care, and earth-care.

Justice is wave that ripples from self-love and as Christiana Figueres said in Moment 81, "systemic change is a deeply personal endeavour."

For me, earth-care begins at home and centers around one word: Consumption.

Consumption of goods.
                        food.
                        energy.
                        water.

Why does earth-care begin at home?

Because home is...

> where routines exist and practices persist.
>
> where dreams germinate and movements begin.
>
> where bread is broke and
>
> where choices are made about what enters our landfills.

Limiting Personal Consumption

Before purchasing something, I ask myself the following questions:

- Have I thought about this purchase for at least 4 weeks?
- Does it solve a problem I've genuinely noticed?
- Can I be productive and happy without it?
- Does buying it support my values and priorities?
- Where will I put this item if I buy it?
- Where will this item be in 5 years?
- Is buying it worth giving up progress towards my next financial goal?
- What is the cost per each use?
- What is my current mental state? (I've noticed myself turn to nonessential consumption if I don't feel grounded. Now I opt for a walk, meditation, or exercise and re-evaluate.)

If I decide I still want to move forward with obtaining the item, I then ask myself:

- Have I checked with a neighbor or my local BUY NOTHING Facebook group?
- Can I craft it myself or buy it used?
- Can I buy it from a local BIPOC-owned business? I avoid shopping at chains and online stores because of the single-use plastics and extra shipping emissions.

Thank you to Abigail at *downsizeupgrade.com* for her thought leadership on mindful consumption.

Next up, Food.

Food is one of the most precious gifts we have in this world and an amazing pathway for deepening our connection with the earth. Below are insights and practices that guide my relationship with food while also considering its impact on the planet.

Mindful Eating
I try to eat slowly, chew thoughtfully, savor each bite, and eat until I'm 80% full. Before I begin eating, I take a moment to consider each individual ingredient and all of the resources, love, and energy that came together for this meal to exist on my plate. I thank the sun and water for the life they support. I thank the people that harvested, processed, packaged, shipped, and stocked the shelves. I thank myself for taking the time to buy, prepare, and cook these nourishing foods.

Cooking
Cooking allows me to maintain better control over portion sizes and ingredient selection. I also find great joy working with my hands and feeling present in the kitchen.

Limiting Meat and Dairy Consumption
The animal product industries consume a massive amount of energy, water, and chemicals to raise animals and the foods they eat. I try to eat vegetarian during the day and when I do eat meat, it's a fun highlight to a meal, not the main event. I especially limit red meat consumption as it has the largest footprint per gram of protein.

Eliminating Waste
- Eat local and seasonal foods to limit the distance that food must travel before reaching your plate.
- Before I go grocery shopping, I always do a quick inventory check to know what I already have and what I need to buy.

This helps limit repeat purchasing.
- At home I'm constantly surveying my cold and dry storage to identify and use "high risk" foods that may expire soon. Freezing, canning, pickling, and fermenting are great ways to manage and save fresh food.
- If I do have food waste or food scraps, I collect them in a countertop bin for composting. If your municipality doesn't offer curbside compost collection, reach out to your local representatives to inquire about one! In the meantime, consider composting at your home or finding a nearby garden that accepts food scraps.

Eating at Restaurants with Intention
- If I do eat out, it is for the experience with friends and to enjoy foods I cannot cook at home. I try to dine-in to avoid the extra packaging required for takeout.
- If I do opt for takeout, I walk or bike to pick up the food myself. Before leaving the restaurant, I make sure no single-use plastics or napkins were placed in the bag as I already have eating utensils at home. I also avoid food delivery companies to ensure more proceeds go directly to the local business.

Next up, energy.
I break this section into two categories, transportation and the home.

Transportation
- Yes to public transportation, walking, and (electric) biking!
- No to self driving and electric cars! While these innovations are a shiny new development from the private car industry, and certainly an improvement from gas-powered cars, it is **not** the solution to our climate crisis. Electric cars often use electricity created from fossil fuels AND the rate of adoption is too slow for the amount of time we have to act. I believe

we must instead focus on creating densely-populated, mixed-use neighborhoods that are walkable, bike-friendly, and connected to public transportation. Changes in zoning codes and the elimination of single-family zoning will create more densely populated neighborhoods that support non-car transportation.

The Home

- Adjust what you're wearing before you adjust the temperature on the thermostat.
- Opt for LED and motion sensor lights to limit electric use
- Purchase dish towels or cut up old fabrics to use instead of paper towels. In my home, we keep one towel for recently washed hands and one towel for wiping countertops.
- Grow your own veggies and herbs if you have the space to do so!

For Current and Future Home Owners

- Stop growing grass! Instead, consider planting native species that require less inputs to maintain.
- When building or renovating a home, consider the sourcing location and chemical makeup of your building materials. For example, spray foam insulation contains toxic chemicals and modern building materials like steel and cement require a lot of energy and water to produce.
- Buy high-efficiency, low water flow, and electric appliance systems. For example, heat pumps regulate the temperature in your home without using natural gas. Check with your municipality about available subsidies.
- Upgrade your windows, doors, and insulation so your home holds its temperature longer.
- Invest in solar panels! While this can be an expensive initial investment, it can often save you money in the long term while also increasing your resiliency from power outages.

Be sure to check with local providers about incentive
programs and financing options that work for your budget.

- When maintaining your roof, opt for lighter colored materials
to reflect the sun's heat and not absorb it.
- If you need to replace your roof, connect with solar panel
providers to explore bundling and financing your roof
purchase with a solar panel system.

Your Journey

Self-care, home-care, and earth-care are all deeply personal and iterative practices. I encourage you to start simple and find what works best for you and your community. Momentum is key and the goal is not self sufficiency, it's **community sufficiency**.

The Unspoken Lever

Individual action is not the only lever we must pull in our fight to save our planet. While it's beyond the direct focus of this book, there is still a pressing need for us to hold corporations, governments, and other large polluters accountable for their impacts to the planet.

Regardless of how you personally decide to engage with the existential threat of our climate crisis, what's most important is that we act with urgency and fight for the future we deserve. Life wants to thrive, we just have to work with it.

And now for the 100th Moment, an original poem titled, Consumption.

Moment 100
Consumption

Consumed by consumption
Where the function
of American holiday functions
Is to buy dumb shit
just to dump it
Credit card pain drain the numbness
We teach our youngins
through screen time
More like fiend time
And soon, they too, share the obsession with material possession
Where's the lesson

~

Guess I'm jaded by extractive obsolescence
and the distracted buying preference
so I'll leave you with a question
Mother Earth's crying soul...

Did We Forget It?

—Jonathan Dean

100 Moments of Media

A Collection of Inspiration and Influences

Books

- A Walk in the Woods by Bill Bryson
- Bhagavad Gita: A New Translation by Stephen Mitchell
- Braiding Sweetgrass by Robin Wall Kimmerer
- Emergent Strategy by Adrienne Maree Brown
- Forest Bathing: How Trees Can Help You Find Health and Happiness by Dr. Qing Li
- Four Thousand Weeks: Time Management for Mortals by Oliver Burkeman
- How to Eat by Thích Nhất Hạnh
- Joyful by Ingrid Fetell Lee
- Kitchen Confidential: Adventures in the Culinary Underbelly by Anthony Bourdain
- Man's Search for Meaning by Viktor Frankl
- On The Road by Jack Keuroac
- Parable of the Sower by Octavia E. Butler
- Parable of the Talents by Octavia E. Butler

- Street Fight by Janet Sadik-Khan
- The Alchemist by Paulo Coelho
- The Creative Act by Rick Rubin
- The Four Agreements: A Practical Guide to Personal Freedom by Don Miguel Ruiz
- The Green Belt Movement: Sharing the Approach and the Experience by Wangari Maathai
- The Nature Fix: Why Nature Makes us Happier, Healthier, and More Creative by Florence Williams
- Triumph of the City by Edward Glaeser
- Walkable City by Jeff Speck
- Zen and the Art of Saving the Planet by Thích Nhất Hạnh

Movies and Documentaries
- 'Before' Trilogy (1995, 2004, 2013)
- Blue Whales 3D: Return of the Giants (2023)
- Brooklyn (2015)
- Can You Ever Forgive Me (2018)
- Chef (2014)
- CODA (2021)
- Dead Poets Society (1989)
- DamNation (2014)
- Erin Brockovich (2000)
- Everything Everywhere All At Once (2022)
- Fantastic Fungi (2019)
- Inside Out (2015)
- KIDS (1995)
- Kiss The Ground (2020)
- Kramer vs. Kramer (1979)
- Mona Lisa Smile (2003)
- Notting Hill (1999)
- Parasite (2019)
- Pretty Woman (1990)
- Ready Player One (2018)

- Residue (2020)
- Super Size Me 2: Holy Chicken! (2017)
- The Biggest Little Farm (2018)
- The Bird Cage (1996)
- The Place Beyond the Pines (2012)

Storytellers on Youtube
- @Channel5YouTube with Andrew Callaghan
- @DiscoverPermaculture with Geoff Lawton
- @ExploringAlternatives
- @happenfilms with Antoinette Wilson & Jordan Osmond
- @JKenjiLopezAlt with J. Kenji López-Alt
- @johnnyharris with Johnny Harris
- @kirstendirksen with Kirsten Dirksen
- @KissTheGround
- @MartijnDoolaard with Martijn Doolaard
- @NotJustBikes with Jason Slaughter
- @ProHomeCooks with Mike Greenfield
- @restorationagriculturedeve4582 with Mark Shepard
- @SavannaInstitute
- @SoulFireFarm
- @TheWeedyGarden with David Trood

Podcasts
- 99% Invisible with Roman Mars
- On Being with Krista Tippett
- Rethink Real Estate. For Good. with Eve Picker
- Ten Percent Happier with Dan Harris
- Tetragrammaton with Rick Rubin
- The Infrastructure Show with Joseph Schofer

Television
- DAVE (2020)
- High Maintenance (2016)

- Last Chance U: Basketball (2021)
- Love (2016)
- Seinfeld (1989)
- Sex and the City (1998)
- The Bear (2022)
- The Undoing (2020)

Albums
- 2014 Forest Hills Drive by J. Cole
- Absolutely by Dijon
- Acid Rap by Chance the Rapper
- American Love Call by Durand Jones & The Indications
- Blonde by Frank Ocean
- Channel Orange by Frank Ocean
- Circles by Mac Miller
- Ctrl by SZA
- For Broken Ears by Tems
- good kid, m.A.A.d city by Kendrick Lamar
- Malibu by Anderson .Paak
- Mirage by Manywellz
- New Blue Sun by André 3000
- No Thank You by Little Simz
- One Wayne G by Mac Demarco
- RAMONA PARK BROKE MY HEART by Vince Staples
- Swimming by Mac Miller
- Telefone by Noname
- The Lost Boy by Cordae
- The Miseducation of Lauryn Hill by Lauryn Hill
- This Is What I Mean by Stormzy
- Voodoo by D'Angelo
- Whack World by Tierra Whack
- xx by The xx

Bibliography

1 (Love Letter Part 3): Rabindranath Tagore. (1975). *Fireflies*. Free Press.

2 Harris, D. H., (Host). (2024, January 3). Esther Perel on the One Thing That Will Improve the Quality of Your Life (No. 705) In *Ten Percent Happier with Dan Harris*. 10% Happier, Inc. https://podcasts.apple.com/us/podcast/ten-percent-happier-with-dan-harris/id1087147821?i=1000639230558

Moment 3: Nhất Hạnh, Thích. (2008). *Being peace*. Read How You Want.

Moment 4: Nhất Hạnh, Thích. (2008). *Being peace*. Read How You Want.

Moment 5: Oliver, M. (2016). *Upstream : select essays*. Penguin Press.

Moment 7: brown, adrienne maree. (2017). *Emergent Strategy*. AK Press.

Moment 12: Gorman, A. (2021). *The hill we climb : an inaugural poem for the country*. Viking Books For Young Readers, An Imprint Of Penguin Random House.

Moment 14: Brown, B. (2017). *Rising strong : how the ability to reset transforms the way we live, love, parent, and lead*. Random House.

Moment 15: Matthew Woodring Stover, & Lucas, G. (2005). *Star wars, episode III. Revenge of the Sith*. Lucas Books/Del Rey.

Moment 19: Franklin, B., & Masur, L. P. (2016). *The Autobiography of Benjamin Franklin : with related documents*. Bedford/St. Martin's, Macmillan Learning.

Moment 26: Angelou, M. (2011). *And Still I Rise*. Random House.

Moment 27: Rubin, R. (2023). *The Creative Act*. Penguin.

Moment 31: *Ten Rules | Corita.org*. (n.d.). Www.corita.org. https://www.corita.org/tenrules

Moment 33: Rubin, R. (2023). *The Creative Act*. Penguin.

Moment 34: Burkeman, O. (2021). *Four Thousand Weeks*. Farrar, Straus and Giroux.

Moment 37: Roosevelt, T. (1913). *Theodore Roosevelt : an autobiography*. The Macmillan Company.

Moment 38: Noel, A. (2009). *Evermore*. St. Martin's Press

Moment 43: Nouwen, H., & Laird, R. (2003). *The Heart of Henri Nouwen*. Crossroad.

Moment 45: Mitchell, S. (2007). *Bhagavad Gita*. Harmony Books.

Moment 47: Butler, O. E. (2023). *Parable of the Sower*. Grand Central Publishing.

Moment 48: Ingrid Fetell Lee. (2020). *Joyful : the surprising power of ordinary things to create extraordinary happiness*. Rider Books.

Moment 49: Thích Nhất Hạnh. (2012). *Living Buddha, Living Christ*. Random House.

Moment 52: Butler, C. (2009). *The Feminine Monarchy: Or the History of Bees (1623)*.

Moment 63: brown, adrienne maree. (2017). *Emergent Strategy*. AK Press.

Moment 65: Clifton, L. (2021). *How to Carry Water: Selected Poems of Lucille Clifton*. Boa Editions, Limited.

Moment 67: Anderson, J. (2014). *All My Loose Ends: Nourish Your Roots*, Jamie Anderson.

Moment 71: Rabindranath Tagore. (1975). *Fireflies*. Free Press.

Moment 73: Rubin, R. (2023). *The Creative Act*. Penguin.

Moment 79: Mead, M. Keys, D. (1985). *Earth at Omega: Passage to*

Planetization. Branden Pub. Co.

Moment 81: Christina Figueres [@CFigueres]. (2023, July 12). *Paradoxically, Systemic Change is a Deeply Personal Endeavour*. [Tweet]. X. https://twitter.com/CFigueres/status/1679047596831043584

Moment 83: Tippett, K. T., (Host). (2023, November 9). Christina Figueres — Ecological Hope, and Spritual Evolution (No. 1,119) In *On Being with Krista Tippett*. The On Being Project. https://podcasts.apple.com/us/podcast/on-being-with-krista-tippett/id150892556?i=1000634295003

Moment 85: Mitchell, S. (2007). *Bhagavad Gita*. Harmony Books.

Moment 91: Heidegger, M. (2008). *Being and Time* (J. Macquarrie & E. Robinson, Trans.). Harperperennial/Modern Thought. (Original work published 1927)

Moment 95: Robin Wall Kimmerer. (2013). *Braiding Sweetgrass: Indigenous Wisdom, Scientific Knowledge and the Teachings of Plants*. Penguin Books.

Contributors and Proceeds

The Contributors

Moment 1: Zoya Yaseka ^

Moment 2: Jonathan Dean

Moment 3: Jonathan Dean

Moment 4: Jonathan Dean

Moment 5: Jonathan Dean

Moment 6: Jonathan Dean

Moment 7: Jonathan Dean

Moment 8: Dan Kershner ^

Moment 9: Jonathan Dean

Moment 10: Chalice Stroebe ^

Moment 11: Mathama B. ^

Moment 12: Sheri Keiles ^

Moment 13: Gia Athanasia ^

Moment 14: Jonathan Dean

Moment 15: Jackson Steger *

Moment 16: Jackson Steger *

Moment 17: Shadman Uddin *

Moment 18: Jamie Lauren Keiles ^

Moment 19: Jonathan Dean

Moment 20: Jonathan Dean

Moment 21: William Tyrone Toms

Moment 22: Melissa Alam ^

Moment 23: Darren Douglas ^

Moment 24: Sebastian De Beurs *

Moment 25: Grant Stopperich ^

Moment 26: Jill Fairchild ^

Moment 27: Jonathan Dean

Moment 28: Garrett Godshall ^

Moment 29: Brunson *

Moment 30: Jonathan Dean

Moment 31: Katy Atherholt ^

Moment 32: Matai Blacklock ^

Moment 33: Jonathan Dean

Moment 34: Jonathan Dean

Moment 35: Jonathan Dean

Moment 36: Bonnie Keiles ^

Moment 37: Mike Wedd ^

Moment 38: Sydney Garfinkel ^

Moment 39: Jonathan Dean

Moment 40: Jonathan Dean

Moment 41: Max Shashoua *

Moment 42: Matt Aragona ^

Moment 43: Jill Fairchild ^

Moment 44: Leonzo Vargas ^

Moment 45: Jonathan Dean

Moment 46: Chalice Stroebe ^

Moment 47: Jonathan Dean

Moment 48: Jonathan Dean

Moment 49: Jonathan Dean

Moment 50: Jonathan Dean

Moment 51: Jonathan Dean

Moment 52: Claire Rater ^

Moment 53: Joe Good ^

Moment 54: Carlos Aponte ^

Moment 55: Bruce Hurowitz ^

Moment 56: Alex Topel ^

Moment 57: Shivam Sabharwal ^

Moment 58: Sly ^

Moment 59: Ethan Asher ^

Moment 60: Kadir Abdi ^

Moment 61: Sherrod Higginbotham ^

Moment 62: Stonez the Organic ^

Moment 63: Jonathan Dean

Moment 64: Nathalie Shapiro *

Moment 65: Chandler Phillips

Moment 66: Jonathan Dean

Moment 67: Jonathan Dean

Moment 68: Jonathan Dean

Moment 69: Carlos Aponte ^

Moment 70: Jonathan Dean

Moment 71: Glen Callahan ^

Moment 72: Jonathan Dean

Moment 73: Jonathan Dean

Moment 74: Cam Lindsay ^

Moment 75: Phyllis Keiles ^

Moment 76: Jonathan Dean

Moment 77: Jonathan Dean

Moment 78: Kow ^

Moment 79: Jonathan Dean

Moment 80: Jonathan Dean

Moment 81: Jonathan Dean

Moment 82: Jonathan Dean

Moment 83: Jonathan Dean

Moment 84: Sarah Kane ^

Moment 85: Jonathan Dean

Moment 86: Jonathan Dean

Moment 87: Josie Bulldozer ^

Moment 88: Abhinav Sridharan ^

Moment 89: Micky Wolf and Anand K. Macherla ^

Moment 90: Micky Wolf and Anand K. Macherla ^

Moment 91: Alex Shandelman

Moment 92: Jonathan Dean

Moment 93: Eric Keiles ^

Moment 94: Phyllis Bergman ^

Moment 95: Ben Sieger ^

Moment 96: Katrina Day ^

Moment 97: Jonathan Dean

Moment 98: Jonathan Dean

Moment 99: Caroline Lutkewitte ^

Moment 100: Jonathan Dean

The Proceeds

Profits from this book are distributed to contributors based on their involvement in the project.

^ = .5% profit share   * = 1% profit share

In addition to the profit distributions for the Moment contributors, profits will also be distributed in the following manner:

- 1% to Dr. Hava Rose for their support with the Idea Gardens
- 2% to Chandler Phillips for their support throughout the project and writing the foreword
- 2% to William Tyrone Toms for his support to the project and the creative community
- 10% to be stewarded by Chandler Phillips to distribute to an organization each year
- 10% to Botanical Dreams. A new organization founded by Jonathan Dean to support ecological restoration projects.

life is a million little moments
enjoyed one at a time

see you on the trail.

love always,
Jonathan Dean

www.ingramcontent.com/pod-product-compliance
Lightning Source LLC
Chambersburg PA
CBHW020237130626
46549CB00005B/1941